V ART™

Animal Hipster

COLORING BOOK

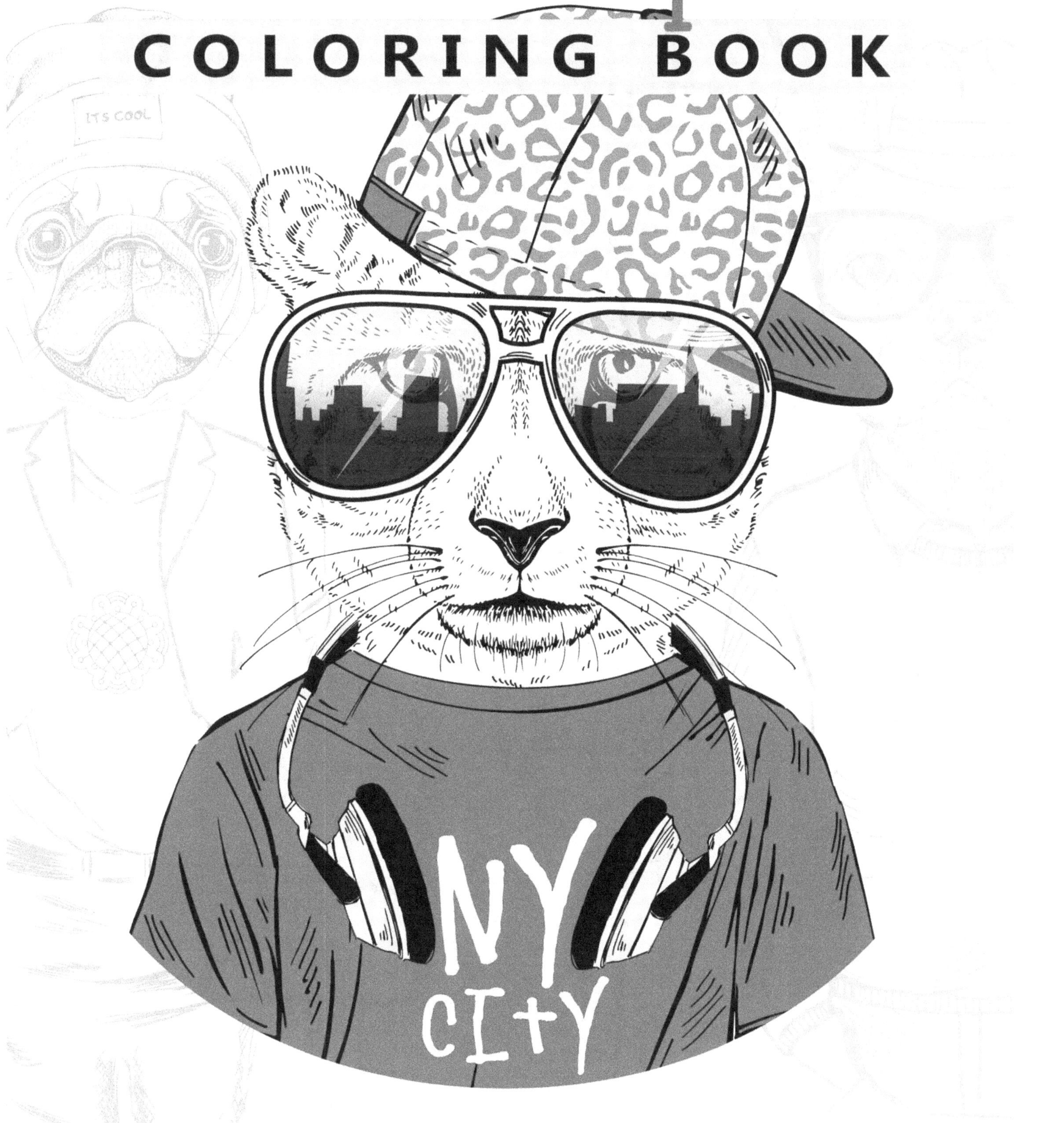

I0414319

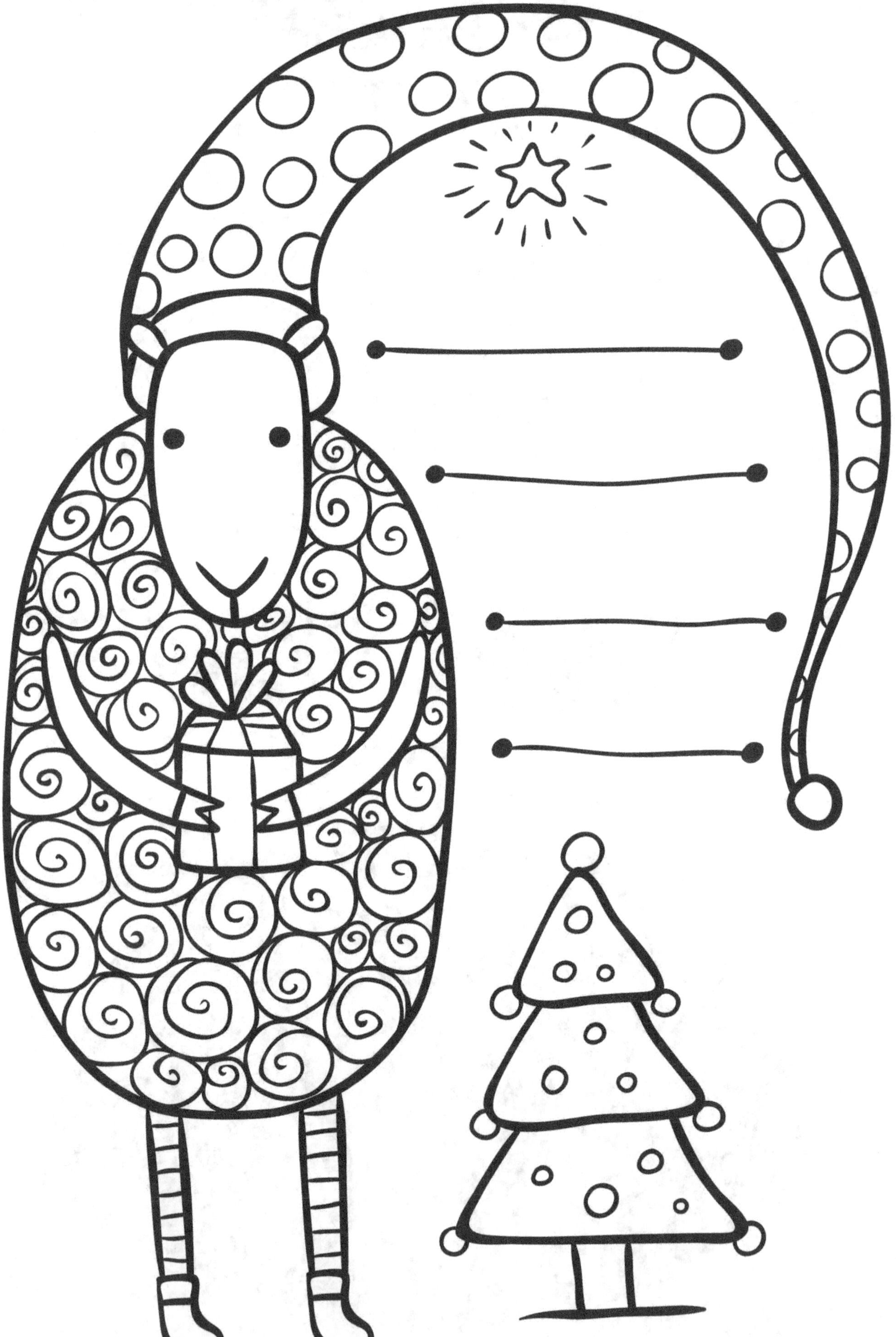

GOOD
VIBES
ONLY
THING
WORTHWHI
COMES
EASI

NO!
love

SAY
«CHEESE»

woof

URBAN
P
PANDA

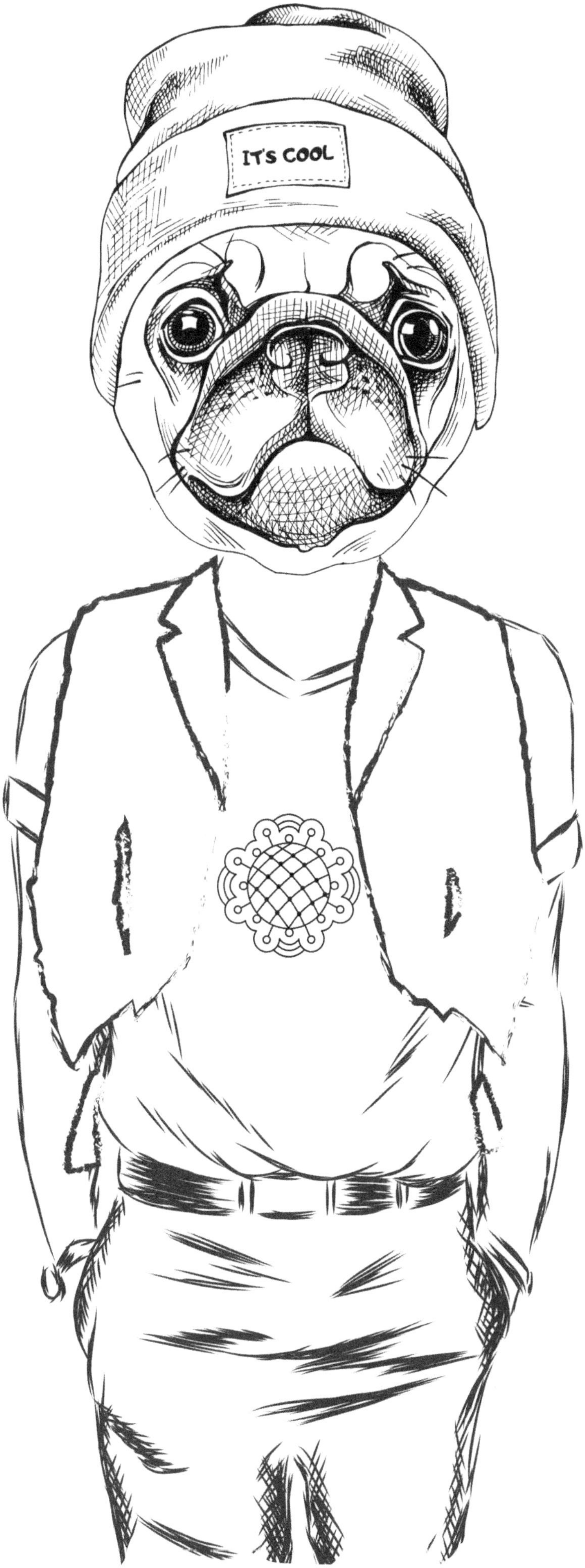
IT'S COOL

YES,
I'M
TRUE

KING

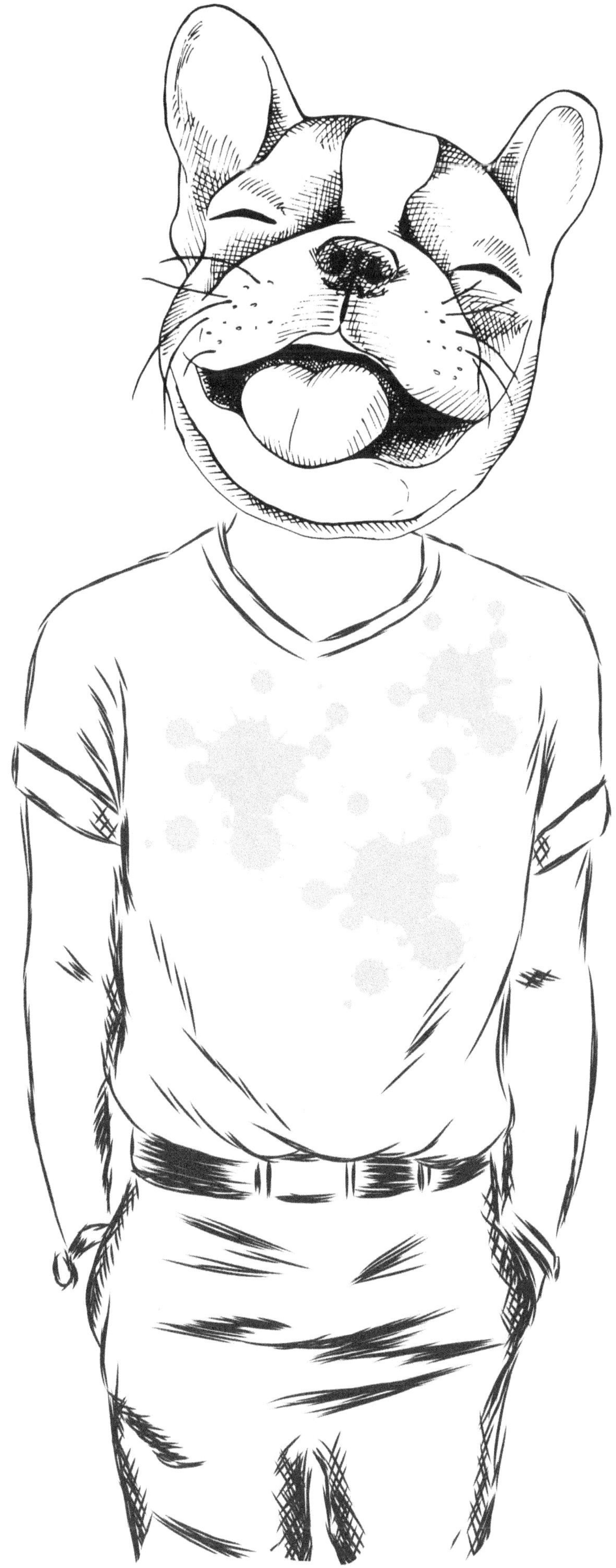

Beardy
and
Brilliant

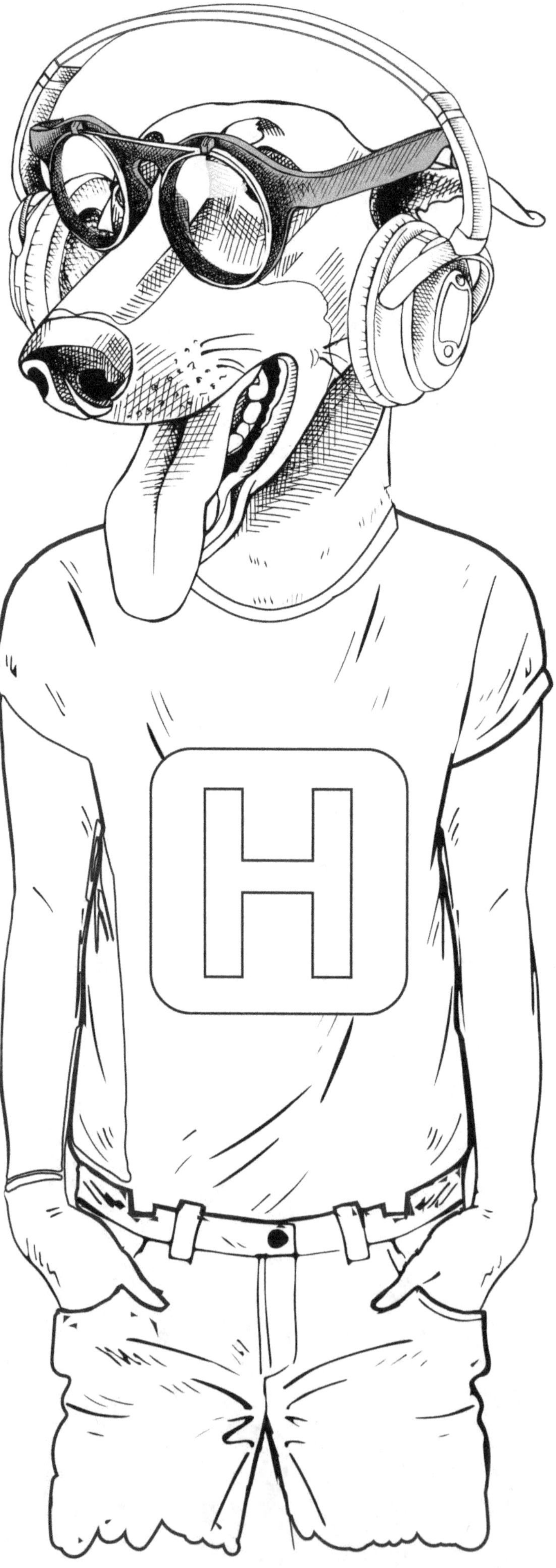
H

Published May 2017

V ART™

www.ingramcontent.com/pod-product-compliance
Lightning Source LLC
Chambersburg PA
CBHW081155280526
45787CB00008B/3333
* 9 7 8 1 5 4 6 8 3 4 7 3 1 *